Biomimicry

Written by **Dora Lee**

Illustrated by **Margot Thompson**

Kids Can Press

For Hayley and Jaime — the world is yours to shape — D.L.

For Neddy — M.T.

Acknowledgments:

Special thanks to Lorne, who believed in me, and to Ken and Alex, who taught me to believe in myself.

Text © 2011 Dora Lee
Illustrations © 2011 Margot Thompson

Kids Can Press acknowledges the financial support of the Government of Ontario, through the Ontario Media Development Corporation's Ontario Book Initiative; the Ontario Arts Council; the Canada Council for the Arts; and the Government of Canada, through the BPIDP, for our publishing activity.

Published in Canada by
Kids Can Press Ltd.
25 Dockside Drive
Toronto, ON M5A 0B5

Published in the U.S. by
Kids Can Press Ltd.
2250 Military Road
Tonawanda, NY 14150

www.kidscanpress.com

The artwork in this book was rendered in acrylic on canvas.
The text is set in Myriad.

Edited by Valerie Wyatt
Designed by Marie Bartholomew

This book is smyth sewn casebound.
Manufactured in Shenzhen, China, in 4/2011 through Asia Pacific Offset

CM 11 0 9 8 7 6 5 4 3 2 1

Library and Archives Canada Cataloguing in Publication

Lee, Dora, 1968–
    Biomimicry : inventions inspired by nature / written by Dora Lee ;

illustrated by Margot Thompson.

Includes index.
ISBN 978-1-55453-467-8

1. Biomimicry—Juvenile literature. 2. Technological innovations—Juvenile literature. I. Thompson, Margot, 1965– II. Title.

T173.8.L44 2011   j608   C2011-900085-7

Kids Can Press is a *corus*™ Entertainment company

Contents

Learning from Mother Nature

Let's give ourselves a pat on the back — we humans have done well for ourselves. From earliest times, we've managed to survive, and even thrive, under harsh conditions. Our inventions have protected us from the weather, provided us with food, shuttled us from place to place and helped us to be healthy. In our battle to tame nature, we've come out on top. Some might call us the most successful species on Earth.

Look around you, though, and you might begin to wonder if we're going about it the right way. As our cities gobble up the wilderness, we destroy the homes of plants and animals. We power our homes, cars and factories with fuel that can't be replaced. In fact, we use resources for just about everything we do — to grow food, to build houses, roads and schools and to make paper to write on. Even taking a drink of water uses resources. While we can't just stop using resources, we can stop using them so quickly.

Somehow, every other species has made this planet its home without destroying it. If they can do it, why can't we?

More and more, people are realizing how much we can learn from nature. Maybe what works in nature will work for us, too. These ideas lie at the heart of biomimicry — "bios" means life and "mimicry" means imitating.

Biomimicry is a way of thinking that encourages scientists, inventors and ordinary people to study nature and use *its* solutions to solve *our* problems. By applying nature's principles, maybe we can find a way for *all* species to thrive on this planet.

Nature thought of it first

Try to think of a human invention that nature didn't come up with first. Not airplanes — they were modeled after birds. Sonar? Long before we came up with the idea, bats bounced sound waves off objects to locate them, a process called echolocation.

It's not surprising that nature beat us to so many of "our" inventions. After all, every other living thing faces the same problems that we do: finding food, water and shelter and protecting itself. Birds probably evolved to fly because flying helped them cover larger areas in search of food or move faster to evade enemies. Bats, active at night, evolved echolocation to help them hunt insects in the dark. Adaptations like these took the right circumstances, a little luck and a lot of time to evolve into such perfect solutions. Let's take a look at some of nature's amazing inventions — after all, they've inspired some of our best ideas.

Bats use echolocation to find and hunt insects at night.

The motor is widely thought to be a uniquely human invention. But when scientists got a close-up view of the inner workings of cells, they got a reality check. Thousands of years before humans even appeared on Earth, nature had already come up with a motor that helped propel bacteria through water. This microscopic motor powers the whipping action of a bacterium's long, threadlike tail. This action pushes water down and behind the bacterium to move it forward.

Today, soldiers wear uniforms and drive vehicles camouflaged to blend in with their surroundings. But animals "invented" camouflage long before we did. For example, an alligator snapping turtle tucks in its limbs to imitate a rock and waves a pink knob of flesh from its tongue like a wiggling worm — perfect for attracting fish at mealtime. Viceroy butterflies look and behave like poisonous monarch butterflies to keep from being eaten. And the spots on baby deer break up the outlines of their bodies, making them hard to "spot."

Velcro is probably the most famous example of biomimicry. More than 40 years ago, Swiss inventor George de Mestral noticed how stubbornly cockleburs clung to his pants. Curious, he examined one of the cockleburs under a microscope. The bur's natural hook like shape and the way it clung to the fabric loops of his pants inspired him to develop his famous two-sided fastener with loops on one side and hooks on the other.

Why should we copy nature?

Armed with the latest and greatest technology, we can design and build just about anything. But will our inventions work and for how long? Nature has had approximately 3.8 billion years' worth of inventing experience. On Earth, the ultimate lab, nature's "experimental models" are continually tested against real-life conditions. What works, stays. What doesn't, goes.

From clusters of molecules to entire ecosystems, nature's inventions are lean, green machines that get the job done. Plus they practically take care of themselves. Chemical and biological signals flow between the parts to make sure that everything is as it should be. When something goes wrong, signals fly back and forth, triggering actions that will either fix the problem or find a way to work around it. No waste. No maintenance. Why *wouldn't* we copy nature?

**The forest floor is an ecosystem —
a sustainable community of plants,
animals and fungi.**

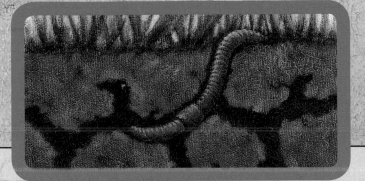

Even in an ordinary patch of soil, millions of living things work together to thrive. Worms tunnel through the soil, letting water and air get to plant roots and soil dwellers, such as insects, fungi and bacteria. Soil creatures eat the worm droppings to get the nutrients they need to do their jobs. They break down dead plants and animals into food for living plants and animals. Each creature has its own part to play in keeping the soil a healthy place to live. This arrangement works because every living thing depends on another: One creature's waste becomes another's food or provides something else an organism needs. City planners, pay attention. This is no ordinary pile of dirt — it's a sustainable community.

If only we could recycle as well as nature does! Even the carbon atoms that make up living things get reused. Here's how it works. A plant adds sunlight and water to convert the carbon dioxide (a form of carbon) in air to sugars that help it grow. A deer eats the plant, turning some of its carbon into muscle. The deer also breathes out carbon dioxide, returning some to the air. Then a wolf eats the deer, taking the deer's carbon into its own body. When the wolf dies, soil organisms break down its body, releasing carbon into the soil to be used by other plants and animals. And so it goes, in the endless loop called the carbon cycle. A carbon atom in your body could have been part of the body of a dinosaur 100 million years ago!

Even our own bodies can teach us something — in fact, they already have. For instance, our kidneys keep tabs on water, salt and other substances in our bodies. Too little water, and the kidneys send a signal to the brain: "Drink something!" Too much water, and they signal: "It's time to pee." The kidneys also sort out salts such as potassium, sodium and phosphorus, keeping only what our bodies need and sending the rest into the waste stream. This is how kidneys keep our blood clean. Our kidneys inspired a doctor to invent an artificial kidney — the dialysis machine — that cleans the blood for patients whose kidneys are damaged.

Pipevine plants know a thing or two about "auto" repair. When a crack develops on the outside of the vine's stem, cells on the inside automatically swell to plug the crack. Then the cells multiply to make more cells to fill up the hole. In young stems, the cell borders thicken up to make the stem stiff. In older stems, the cell walls stay soft, so the vine can wrap itself around supports as it grows. Scientists are working on a kind of foam that mimics the pipevine's cells. They hope to use it on a new type of building beam that is filled with air to make it light yet strong. In case of an air leak, the foam would swell and plug the hole to prevent the beam's collapse.

Why are lotus flowers always spotlessly clean? Tiny hydrophobic (water-repelling) bumps cover the leaves and petals. Water sits on top of the waxy bumps instead of filling in the nooks and crannies between them. So do particles of dirt. When it rains, water drops roll off the leaves and flowers, picking up the dirt as they go. Recently, scientists have mimicked this "lotus effect" by spiking paint with microscopic water-repellent bumps that let dirt roll off walls with the rain.

The giant reed has spongy stems that bend but rarely break, thanks to bundles of stiff fibers running along the length of each stem. Another weed, the giant horsetail (right), has a hollow stem that's incredibly strong because it's made of two layers held apart by braces. Scientists are combining these characteristics to make a human-made material that's both flexible and strong. One day, this new material may be used in aircraft, vehicles, buildings and sports equipment.

Termites air-condition their mounds by catching the wind in a trench at the mound's base. The air flows through cool mud channels up into tunnels that lead to the top of the mound. Warming as it rises, the air takes the heat with it when it exits the mound at the top. In the 1990s, engineers constructing a building in Zimbabwe achieved the same effect by using big fans to bring cool air into the building at night. During the day, small fans blow the cool air into the rooms. As the air warms, it rises up and out through chimneys poking up from the roof like stems.

The shape and structure of maple seeds help them travel away from their parent tree, making it more likely that they'll find a good place to land and sprout. NASA has proposed to develop aircraft modeled on maple seeds for planetary exploration. These "seed wing flyers" could be released into the atmosphere from a probe flying over the planet's surface. Then, as the flyers twirl down to the planet's surface, they could collect data and relay it back to the probe before landing.

Shaped for survival

Attention, architects and engineers — the perfect design might be right outside your window. Take a bee's honeycomb, for example. It's constructed of hexagonal (six-sided) cylinders because this shape uses the smallest amount of beeswax to produce the most space for storing honey. Over thousands, even millions of years, nature made tiny improvements to the honeycomb to maximize space and minimize the amount of beeswax needed.

We don't have millions of years to tinker with our inventions — not if we want to be alive to use them. So it makes sense for us to take advantage of nature's experience. After all, nature's shapes and structures have already withstood the test of time. As these examples show, scientists and inventors are already borrowing from the natural world.

Bees build a honeycomb that maximizes honey storage and minimizes materials.

Smart structures

What does "being smart" mean? If it means reacting in a logical way to what your senses tell you, then humans and animals are definitely smart. But what about plants, bacteria or fungi? They don't think, but they do have ways of sensing and responding to changes in their environment.

Some of these organisms can sense light, moisture or certain chemicals and move or turn toward them. Snow buttercups, for example, turn their faces to the sun every day and follow it from east to west across the sky. Other living things have structures that act as if they "know" what is happening around them and can "decide" what to do. The Venus flytrap, for example, snaps shut when it "feels" an insect tickling two or more hairs on its leaf.

Many living things evolve parts or behaviors that perfectly suit the environment that they live in. These strategies aren't the result of conscious thinking. Instead, they work because trial and error over many generations has fine-tuned them into "smart structures" that respond in specific ways to specific triggers. Increasingly, scientists are turning to structures in nature to find clues that will help us create our own smart structures. The results, so far, are encouraging.

Snow buttercups sense the sun and turn their blossoms to follow it.

At the 2000 Summer Olympic Games in Sydney, Australia, 28 of the 33 gold medal winners in swim events wore sharkskin-inspired swimsuits. Why? The structure of a shark's skin reduces turbulence — the churned-up water that makes for slow swimming. Tiny, grooved scales cover the shark's skin. The scales are lined up so that the grooves form continuous channels along the shark's body. Normally, water becomes turbulent when it crashes against a swimming object, such as a shark. But the channels of grooves straighten out the turbulent water, making it easier for the shark to swim through.

If nature can produce colors without pigments — often made from toxic chemicals — so can we. The wings of blue Morpho butterflies get their beautiful blue color from the layers of transparent structures that make up their scales. Each layer reflects blue light at a specific angle. The combined effect is layer upon layer of blue light waves striking our eyes. We don't just see *blue*, we see *blue plus blue plus blue* — an intense, iridescent blue. One textile company in Japan decided to "wing it" and developed a shimmery fabric woven from fibers of different thicknesses layered to reflect light the same way as the blue Morpho's wing scales.

How do pinecones know when to open up their scales so their seeds can fall out? Their scales are made up of two layers. When it's wet out, the outer layer absorbs water more quickly and swells to keep the scale shut. When it's dry out, the outer layer loses water and shrinks, pulling the scale open. This lets the seed pop out during the dry season, when the wind can blow it farther from its parent tree. Inspired by this simple yet effective technique, researchers have developed a fabric with flaps that open when you sweat so you can cool down and close again when you dry off.

The corpse lily, whose fleshy flowers smell like rotting meat, doesn't stink for nothing — its odor attracts flies that pollinate the plant. Now here's a challenge for you: Can you invent a way that humans could use the corpse lily's smelly strategy to solve one of our own problems?

13

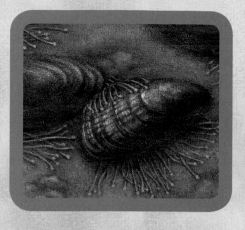

To keep the tide from washing them away, blue mussels anchor themselves to rocks with homemade tethers called byssal threads. Each byssal thread is covered with a special coating that protects it from crashing waves and hungry microbes. After a few years, the coating falls apart so the byssal thread can decompose. Scientists are trying to develop a similar coating that protects items while we use them but wears off after several years, allowing the items to degrade instead of taking up space in our landfills.

Most plastics use nonrenewable resources — gas, crude oil or coal — as starting materials. Turning these materials into plastic takes a lot of energy. Plus, most plastics take forever to break down. A new plastic might change all that. Made from carbon dioxide and an oil from orange peels, this plastic starts with renewable materials and takes very little energy to make, thanks to a special chemical that kick-starts the manufacturing process. Best of all, producing this new plastic uses up carbon dioxide that might otherwise contribute to global warming.

Nacre, the iridescent lining of an abalone shell, is mostly calcium carbonate, which is plain old chalk. But nacre is so tough that a truck can drive over a shell without cracking it. What stops cracks in their tracks is the way nacre is built, brick-and-mortar style. The "bricks" are hard but would crumble if a protein "mortar" didn't hold them together. The abalone somehow assembles its shell without using heat, complex equipment or chemicals. Scientists are trying to figure how, so that they too can create superstrong materials under ordinary conditions.

Magic materials

Natural materials such as wood, silk, wool and bone look different, feel different and are used in different ways. But they do have a few things in common. They're created by environmentally friendly processes that use ordinary materials such as water. When they've served their purpose, these materials decompose, returning to the earth.

Human-made materials are the exact opposite. We make synthetic materials such as plastic and nylon by "heat, beat and treat" processes. We melt, fuse or squeeze materials under heat and high pressure, or carve and shape them using harsh chemicals. When synthetic materials were first invented, people marveled at how durable they were. Now we realize that's exactly what we don't want — materials so long lasting that when we discard them, they stay in our landfills forever. Can we make materials that behave more naturally, using processes more like nature's?

The wood in a tree trunk is made by the tree itself, using only water and sunlight. When the tree dies, the wood decays, releasing nutrients. Sometimes the decomposing tree becomes a "nurse tree" for a new tree.

Creative communications

Humans have devised ingenious ways of capturing information and transmitting it over long distances. Communications technology has progressed from cave drawings to telephones, e-mail and fiber optics. Some of these inventions, such as the telephone or DVD player, don't seem to have any connection to nature, but others might not exist if it weren't for nature's inspiration. For example, a camera works like a human eye. A diaphragm in the camera changes the amount of light that enters the camera in the same way the iris of a human eye changes the size of the pupil to control how much light gets into the eye.

Of course, humans aren't the only ones who can pass information along to others. For instance, many animals communicate with specific signals. A wolf, realizing that it's about to lose a fight, signals "I give up" by rolling over to expose its throat and belly. Baby herring gulls signal "feed me!" by pecking at the red spot on a parent's beak. As scientists delve deeper into the way other living organisms communicate, they're making new discoveries that promise to change the way we communicate in the future.

A baby herring gull pecks the red spot on its parent's beak to signal "I want food!"

Squid change their skin color to hide from predators, surprise their prey or just talk among themselves. They owe this ability to special pigment-filled sacs under their skin called chromatophores. When a squid contracts muscles surrounding a chromatophore, it opens, showing the color inside. When it relaxes those muscles, the chromatophore closes, shrinking to expose an iridescent layer of cells underneath. The pattern of open and closed chromatophores determines the patterns and colors that show up on the squid's skin. Some electronic billboards and e-books use the same principle. A pattern of exposed microcapsules, filled with either black or white particles, forms the letters of the message that appears.

Several hundred million years before we came up with the idea, ancient sea sponges used fiber optics to collect light from the ocean floor and beam it to other sea sponges. Nicknamed the Venus flower basket, the sponge is surrounded by a mineral cage fringed with fine whiskers. The whiskers are made of the same material that we make high-tech fiber optic cables out of — with one important difference. Inside each of the sponge's whiskers is a thread of protein. Scientists believe that this protein may be the key to improving our own fiber optic technology.

Modern underwater communication devices send and receive information using sound waves — it's a bit like radio, only under water. But the signal scatters if it has to travel too far because noises and echoes from boats, machinery and sea creatures interfere. Dolphins, however, have no problem communicating over long distances. It turns out that singing is the key. By continuously changing the pitch of their voices from very high to very low, dolphins can separate their signals from other sounds that interfere with their messages. One underwater communications company mimicked dolphin sound patterns to develop modems that separate the information-containing sound waves from other noises in the water. This way, data can be transmitted over much longer distances.

Our cells are covered in a layer, made mostly of fat, called the cell membrane. Scientists are working on artificial fat bubbles called liposomes that mimic this membrane. Liposomes can be filled with drugs and injected into the body to fight disease. Because they look like real cells from the outside, the liposomes can sneak past the body's defenses and "melt" into diseased cells, such as cancer cells, where they release their drug payload. Without this fatty disguise, drugs entering the body would be recognized as foreign and attacked by the body's immune system before they could do their work.

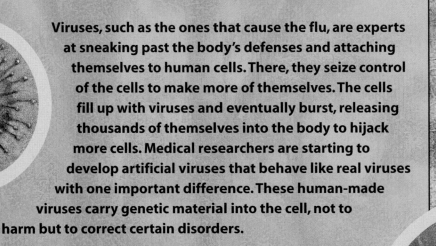

Viruses, such as the ones that cause the flu, are experts at sneaking past the body's defenses and attaching themselves to human cells. There, they seize control of the cells to make more of themselves. The cells fill up with viruses and eventually burst, releasing thousands of themselves into the body to hijack more cells. Medical researchers are starting to develop artificial viruses that behave like real viruses with one important difference. These human-made viruses carry genetic material into the cell, not to harm but to correct certain disorders.

Battling bacteria usually means attacking them with antibiotics. But a few of the strongest bacteria always survive. They (and their descendants) can't be killed by antibiotics — they've become antibiotic resistant. This has researchers scrambling to find new ways to control bacteria. Their quest has led them to red seaweed — one of the few organisms on which biofilms never form. Biofilms are mats of bacteria that grow when a few bacteria send a chemical message inviting more bacteria to join them. But red seaweed sends a fake message — call it seaweed spam — to take the place of the real message. The real message never gets through, so the biofilm never forms. Copying red seaweed's strategy, scientists are crafting chemical messages that they hope will prevent biofilms of bacteria from forming on other surfaces, too.

Some of our most powerful medicines have come from plants. But finding which plants have medicinal properties takes time. So far, we've managed to test only about 5000 of more than 300 000 known plants. Recently, though, some scientists are taking shortcuts, courtesy of nature. They observe chimpanzees and note which plants sick chimps seek out, then zero in on these plants for testing.

Medical marvels

Living things have an amazing capacity to defend themselves against germs, fight disease and repair damage that's done to them. The pipevine's remarkable ability to plug cracks in its stem is only one example (see page 9). Trees respond to wounds and pruning cuts by forming walls around the damaged areas. These walls keep organisms that rot wood from spreading into the healthy tree. Eventually, a lumpy callus grows over the dead wood.

Our bodies, like those of all animals, have a powerful army that defends them against invaders — the immune system. Think of what a germ has to go through to make you sick. First, it has to get past your skin. If it manages to sneak in through a cut or scratch, it has to dodge the specialized cells that patrol your body, seeking out and destroying germs before they can take over healthy cells. And even if a germ gets this far, the immune system still has ways to help your body fight it.

Understanding how your body protects itself has helped doctors and scientists devise inventive ways to combat diseases and infections. Sometimes this means using knowledge gained from nature to get around nature's own defenses.

This tree surrounded a damaged area with a callus.

On the move

In the late 1400s, Leonardo da Vinci did detailed drawings that showed his understanding of bird and mechanical flight. Many of his drawings included flying machines operated by pilots who used their arms or legs to flap birdlike wings. In the nineteenth and twentieth centuries, German engineer Otto Lilienthal and the American brothers Orville and Wilbur Wright also studied birds in flight. Those studies eventually led to the first successfully controlled airplane flight — the Wright brothers' famous flight at Kitty Hawk in 1903.

Not all transportation takes its inspiration from nature — but maybe it should. Engineers are beginning to realize that a closer look at nature's solutions could help us work out the bugs in our own designs.

Birds inspired humans to design flying machines that eventually led to today's airplanes.

When the wind picks up, tumbleweeds start rolling. Rolling helps them travel smoothly over just about any terrain. NASA is working on tumbleweed-shaped rovers (robotic planetary exploration vehicles). During recent tests in Antarctica, the rovers successfully tumbled over rocks and hills and out of pits and craters. They're destined for Mars, where rough terrain defeats ordinary rovers with wheels.

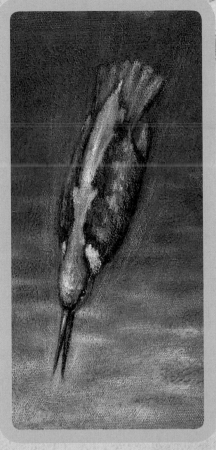

Scrape your knee, and the blood starts flowing. Your body wants to stop the bleeding, so special cells called platelets rush to the wound site and stick together, forming a clot that dries into a scab. Underneath the scab, brand new skin grows. Now scientists have copied the healing process — for airplanes. They've invented a new plastic material that will let a damaged plane "heal" itself. This new plastic has tiny tubes embedded in it, some filled with epoxy (a glue) and some filled with a hardening agent. When the plastic is damaged — for instance, in a crash — the tubes break. The materials ooze out of the tubes, mix and harden, temporarily sealing the crack and allowing the plane to fly safely home for more permanent repairs.

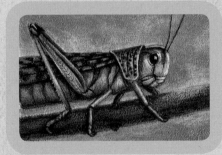

Swarming insects fly wing to wing but rarely hit each other, or anything else. The African locust sweeps the area in front of it with a built-in detector behind its eyes. A bee's compound eyes scan even more space — almost 360 degrees. Both insects send a signal to change direction the instant they detect an obstacle. Could insects teach car makers something about collision avoidance? In the future, cars could have systems that can detect and automatically steer away from oncoming objects, without driver input.

One of the world's fastest trains, the Shinkansen, or bullet train, travels between Tokyo and Hakata at speeds of up to 300 km/h (186 m.p.h.). Early bullet trains were noisy. Because they moved so fast through tunnels, a cushion of air built up in front of them. When they burst out of a tunnel, the compressed air rapidly expanded, causing thunderlike booms that were heard long distances away. Kingfishers experience the same sudden change in air pressure when they dive into water to catch fish. The change should result in a huge splash, yet these birds enter the water without a ripple. Engineers changed the front end of the train to look like a kingfisher's long, pointy beak, so it could "slice" through the air in a more streamlined way. The new bullet trains were not only quieter — they required less energy to operate.

The first major underwater tunnel, below the Thames River in London, England, was made possible by a chance encounter between a shipworm and engineer Isambard Brunel. Early attempts at digging a tunnel had failed because the walls kept collapsing. Brunel noticed how the shipworm scraped away wood with a hard shell that also shielded its soft head. Then it deposited lime around the freshly dug hole to hold the dirt in place. This, Brunel realized, was the way to build a tunnel — an iron shield would protect his diggers from falling dirt, while a layer of bricks, laid down as soon as a section was dug, would keep the walls from collapsing.

Less than 2.5 cm (1 in.) of rain falls on the Namib Desert in Africa each year, so every drop counts. The Namib beetle collects the fog that rolls in at night by lowering its head to tilt its shell like a slide. Tiny hydrophilic (water-loving) bumps on the shell attract the drops of fog, and hydrophobic (water-hating) valleys between bumps push the drops together into heavy beads that slide down the beetle's back and into its mouth. To collect water in dry areas of the world, engineers envision making tents and even buildings from materials that mimic the beetle's shell.

When a tornado spins or a peregrine falcon dives after its prey, it moves in a spiral pattern. Spirals, so common in nature, inspired engineers to put a new spin on fan, mixer and turbine blades. These blades are designed to push or pull liquids or air in a spiral instead of the usual straight line. The spiral-inspired blades are more energy efficient and a lot quieter than other blades.

A hornbeam leaf is huge compared to its tiny leaf bud. How did nature cram the big leaf into its small case? The leaf folds up, following angled pleats that line the leaf. Scientists hope to use the same folding technique to pack solar panels into packages small enough to launch into space. Once in space, the panels would open up again to provide lots of surface area to collect solar energy.

Designs that work

Each plant, animal and insect is a marvel of engineering perfected over almost 4 billion years. Every living thing has evolved to function in the way that best helps it to survive, no matter how bizarre it may look to us. Nature's designs result in feats humans can only dream of accomplishing: fireflies that make their own light, frogs that freeze in winter and come back to life each spring and birds that navigate without compasses or maps.

Who knows if our inventions will ever match nature's best? But if we combine nature's designs with our understanding of the science behind them, we can come pretty close.

Fireflies produce light in their bodies through a chemical reaction.

Pollution-free power

Fossil fuels — oil, natural gas and coal — were created millions of years ago. Once they're used up, they can't be replaced. But that's not the only problem with fossil fuels. When coal and oil are burned, they produce greenhouse gases, such as carbon dioxide, that contribute to global warming and generate acid rain and pollution, which can damage our health and our planet. Burning natural gas produces fewer emissions, but it still contributes to climate change. What we really need is a different source of energy.

We've made a start by developing "green" technologies to make energy from renewable resources such as wind, waves, sunlight and hydrogen. But the amount of useful energy we get from these sources isn't great enough to be worth the cost of producing it. So for now, these energy sources stay on the sidelines.

Before green energy can be widely used, we need to find cheaper, more effective ways to generate it. That's why scientists are turning to nature, which generates enough energy to run the whole natural world without burning a drop of oil or emitting a particle of pollution.

With hydroelectric dams, we've already shown we can harness the power of falling water. Can we capture the energy in waves, wind and sunlight, too?

As a fuel, hydrogen is ideal. Burn it under the right conditions and the only emissions are heat and water vapor. Right now, most of our hydrogen comes from natural gas, a fossil fuel, so we can't claim that it's 100 percent green. But greener hydrogen technology may be on its way, thanks to blue-green bacteria. These ancient microbes can extract hydrogen from water using only sunlight for energy and an enzyme called hydrogenase to help the reaction along. Some scientists are looking at ways to use the bacteria to produce hydrogen for them, while others are trying to make their own versions of the enzyme.

You only have to watch ocean waves pound against a cliff to know how much power is stored there. The hard part is harnessing this energy. The secret? You have to go with the flow, using an energy-collecting device that looks and acts like kelp. The device is firmly secured to the seabed by a base modeled after a kelp's holdfast, a root-like structure that keeps the kelp anchored on the ocean floor. The blades of the device float underneath the waves like fronds of kelp, absorbing energy as they move. The energy is transmitted to a generator inside the device to produce electricity.

The wind's power is transferred to a windmill as its blades rotate. But if the wind blows too fast or too slow, the blades stop moving. This is called stalling. Fortunately, nature has also faced this problem and solved it. For example, a humpback whale risks stalling when it turns sharply. But this doesn't happen, thanks to a row of bumps along the front edge of its fins, which helps the whale make a smooth turn. Scientists, learning from humpbacks, have found that adding bumps to the blades of wind turbines and fans makes them less likely to stall.

Dealing with the tough stuff

There's plenty in nature to inspire us in our everyday lives. But knowing how nature deals with extreme conditions could benefit us, too. This information could help us develop materials that work under extreme cold or heat, or show us how to survive hostile environments as we venture out to explore other planets.

Nature has lots of experience with extreme conditions and the creatures that live in them. Get ready to meet the extremophiles, living things that love to live in places that would kill us. The word "extremophile" comes from "extreme" and the Greek word for "lover." For example, *thermophiles* thrive in boiling water, *psychrophiles* like it cold and *halophiles* hanker after salt. Extremophiles are nature's superheroes — able to take the tough stuff — and we've got a lot to learn from them.

These rock formations on the ocean floor are called black smokers. They belch out superhot chemicals that would kill most life, but not the thermophilic bacteria that live in the smokers. They love the heat.

Tardigrades are microscopic water creatures that look like miniature teddy bears. They're also some of the most amazing animals in the world. Tardigrades live in water droplets just about everywhere. If the water dries up, the tardigrades shrivel up into little balls called tuns and live in suspended animation until it gets wet again. Tuns can also withstand crushing pressures, no oxygen, X-rays, temperatures of over 100°C (200°F) and down to −200°C (−300°F). Tardigrades produce a sugar called trehalose that helps them dry up without dying. Imagine if a sprinkle of this sugar could help us preserve medicines and organs for transplants or keep us alive during long trips into space!

In some caves in Mexico, the air smells like rotten eggs, and yellow gobs of something wet and slimy hang down from the vaulted ceiling. Called snottites, these gobs are actually communities of bacteria. And while they do look a lot like snot, that's not the reason they fascinate scientists. Snottite bacteria gobble up poisonous hydrogen sulfide gas and use it for energy, producing sulfuric acid as waste. Why don't the cave gases and burning acid kill the bacteria? Scientists are trying to find out. The answer could help us find ways to explore planets with poisonous atmospheres or clean up toxic waste.

In winter, wood frogs hide under leaves and sometimes freeze solid. In the spring, the frogs thaw and hop around like nothing ever happened. How do they do it? When the cold weather comes, the frogs ramp up production of a sugar called glucose in their bodies, which keeps sharp ice crystals from punching holes in their cells. Scientists wonder if glucose could lengthen the life of cells in transplant organs, too. At present, donated organs, such as hearts and kidneys, have to be used within hours or they stop functioning. Does that mean that someday we'll be able to freeze our bodies to be revived in the future? Sorry, but most scientists agree that's the stuff of science fiction.

In 1969, scientists discovered thermophilic bacteria living in the steaming hot springs of Yellowstone National Park. Years later, scientists used a heat-resistant enzyme from this bacteria to create millions of copies of DNA from as little as a single molecule. Before this discovery, scientists could not easily copy DNA because the heat needed to do so destroyed most enzymes. Now, the technique makes it possible to copy even a tiny bit of DNA. This means, for example, that a tiny sample of DNA evidence from a crime scene can be copied many times. These copies give police enough sample to compare the crime scene DNA to that of the suspects. An exact match could solve the crime.

Computing, nature's way

Who invented computers? Nature, naturally. Living things have been "computing" for as long as they've existed. They collect data, process information, make decisions and act on those decisions to run the processes that keep them alive.

Living things have computing power that human-made computers just can't match. Hundreds of thousands of neurons (nerve cells) firing simultaneously in their brains give organisms the edge. A human-made computer depends instead on transistors for computing power, which is measured as the number of operations per second. One way to increase this power is to add more transistors to a computer chip — the more, the better. But as we rapidly approach the point where we just can't cram any more transistors onto a silicon chip, scientists are turning to nature for ideas. They're looking at atoms, molecules and chemical reactions to help them create new computers based on nature's blueprints.

Nerve cells in the human brain called neurons pass information from one to another.

At 330 trillion operations per second, a biological computer devised in Israel is 100 000 times faster than the fastest personal computer (PC). This Israeli computer, however, looks nothing like your PC. It looks like water. One drop of this clear solution contains a trillion molecules of DNA and enzymes. Just as our computers read and carry out program code to get results, the biological computer uses enzymes to read and process information encoded in the DNA to get its results. But don't recycle that PC yet. Biological computers may be fast — their speed comes from sheer numbers — but they're still very limited in what they can do. At least for now.

Diatoms are single-celled creatures surrounded by lacy, patterned shells. The shells are made of silica — a form of the same material that computer chips are made of. Recently, scientists figured out which genes control the diatom's shell-building process. This is the first step toward understanding how diatoms construct their shells. Once they understand the process, scientists hope to come up with a way to copy it, so they can build silicon computer chips without using toxic chemicals and high temperatures.

The future of ultrafast photonic computers (computers that run on light instead of electricity) may rest on the back of a Brazilian beetle. The scales on the beetle's shell are made up of crystals arranged in such a way that only certain wavelengths of light, and not others, can penetrate them. This makes the beetle appear iridescent green from all angles. Computer scientists think that a similar arrangement of crystals could be used to channel light in photonic computers.

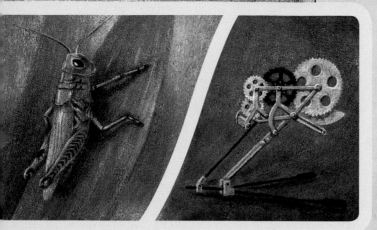

Imagine grasshoppers and cockroaches hopping and scurrying over Mars — scientists have. Mars is full of craters and boulders, which make it difficult for robots on wheels to get around. Robots that jump or scramble, however, would be perfect. Inspired by the natural spring in a grasshopper's leg, a team of scientists created a robot that weighs less than a paper clip and can jump 27 times its own height. Other researchers copied the cockroach. Like the real thing, the robotic cockroach has six powerful legs and a low center of gravity to help it climb obstacles without slowing down.

Finding victims buried under earthquake rubble or trapped in a burning building would be easy for a snake. Snakes can wiggle over, under or around tight spots to get places human rescuers can't. But snakes aren't the most reliable scouts. Instead of using real snakes, engineers are designing robots inspired by snakes. These robots are jointed, so they can slither from side to side like snakes. Sensors in the robot's head and skin help it to avoid obstacles, and because it travels low to the ground, it doesn't tip over or get stuck.

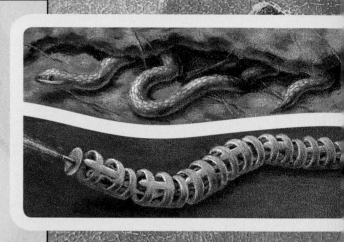

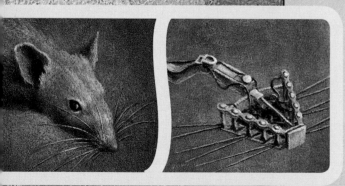

Robots can stop or change direction when they run into something, but it's far better to avoid bumping into things in the first place. So scientists have turned to rats for help. Rats find their way around in dark places by sweeping their whiskers back and forth to gather information about nearby objects or obstacles. Robotics experts are working on sensors that imitate rat whiskers. These mechanical "whiskers" will help a robot sense where an object is, judge how close it is and get information about its size, shape and texture.

Bug wings are causing a flap in robotics circles. Scientists are trying to design robots with flapping wings so that the robots can swivel, hover and take off without a runway. These tiny robotic bugs, called micro-air vehicles (MAVs), could be used to search under rubble for earthquake survivors or spy on terrorist operations. One day, MAVs might even scout the surface of Mars, something that regular aircraft can't do — Mars's thin atmosphere makes it hard for ordinary airplanes to get airborne.

Machines that move like animals ...

Can you explain what a robot is? Chances are you'd have trouble coming up with an exact definition. Here's what the experts say: A typical robot can sense its environment and decide how to interact with it using automatic controls or programmed sequences. It can also move itself or a part of itself without human help.

In old science fiction books, television shows and movies, robots often looked and acted like humans or animals. But in real life, it's difficult to create a robot that convincingly mimics a human or animal. Robotics engineers find it a real challenge to make robots do even simple things, such as picking up a pencil. To make robots move more naturally, they study insects and animals and their moving parts. Then they apply what they've learned to make robots that sense, move and interact with the environment more like living things.

Designing a robotic hand that can move like yours does is one goal of roboticists.

... and think like humans

Robots with personality were once found only in fiction. In real life, robots didn't need to be like humans. They carried out work that was too dangerous or too boring for people to do and, usually, they worked alone.

But times are changing. From robo-vacuums to robo-pets, robots are becoming part of the household. Will it only be a matter of time before every house has a robot? And robots are even being used in hospitals and care homes to provide therapy or companionship. These are known as social robots.

Because social robots deal with people, they need to behave like people — to smile when people around them are happy, or back off when people are upset, for instance. So, taking cues from nature, scientists are studying the way children learn and people interact to help them develop realistic robots that respond appropriately to humans in everyday situations.

What can babies teach robots? Plenty. Computer scientists have been studying babies to see how they learn. In one project, researchers filmed babies playing peekaboo and other games with their mothers. Millisecond by millisecond, the researchers are analyzing the babies' movements and reactions. Then they'll use this information to develop programs to engineer similar behaviors in robots.

Can robots tell if you're happy or sad? Scientists who are participating in the Feelix Growing project are developing robots that can sense emotions and respond to them. Cameras and sensors inside the robots detect signs of emotion in a nearby human, such as facial expressions, changes in voices and head and hand movements. The robots' computer software mimics the way our nerves and brains work to help them learn how to respond to these feelings. If someone shows fear, the robots learn to back away. If someone smiles, the robots learn to smile back or move closer.

Many children with autism have difficulty dealing with people but are fascinated by mechanical devices. This is where lifelike robots, which have characteristics of both, can help. These robots can communicate and respond to human speech and movements — and maybe help autistic children become more comfortable with real people.

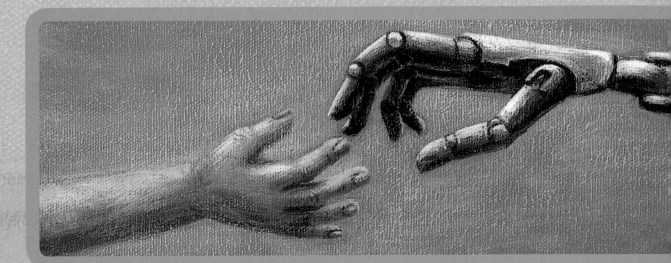

 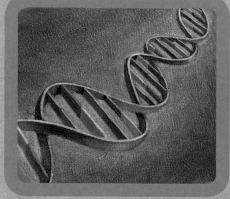 

Proteins are the ultimate nanomachines. Inside your body, they carry out many of the tasks that keep you alive. Proteins are flexible chains of amino acids linked together in such a way that they automatically fold up into the exact shape needed to carry out their task. Chemists have long dreamed of using nature's protein-making process to custom design their own proteins for medical and industrial uses. They've had some luck in copying nature's method for stringing amino acids together into a protein, but they're still working on how to get their synthetic proteins to fold into the exact shape they want.

DNA is a great building material for nanotechnology. Each strand of DNA is strung together from four bases (parts) called A, G, C and T, for short. Each base is attracted to a specific partner — A to T, and G to C. When a base finds its partner, it sticks to it. This is what forms the double-stranded twisted ladder of DNA in all your cells. Scientists can now string bases together to make short strands of DNA in beakers or test tubes. These strands of DNA stick to other DNA pieces to form squares, crosses or other arrangements. These structures can also be cut and pasted together to create three-dimensional structures that have lots of potential uses. Someday, they might hold larger molecules in place or form parts of nano-sized mechanical devices.

Geckos can cling to ceilings because their feet are covered with millions of nano-sized hairs. Each of these hairs branches out into billions of tiny projections called spatulae. Each spatula is only weakly attracted to individual molecules of the ceiling's surface, but billions of them create a powerful bond. If an elephant's feet had enough spatulae, the attraction would be strong enough to stick the elephant to the ceiling, too. Scientists are working on developing "gecko tape," sticky strips with tiny projections a few nanometers long that mimic the hairs on a gecko's foot. Someday, this nanomaterial may be used in skin grafts to replace stitches that close wounds, and even to make climbing robots that can scramble up walls.

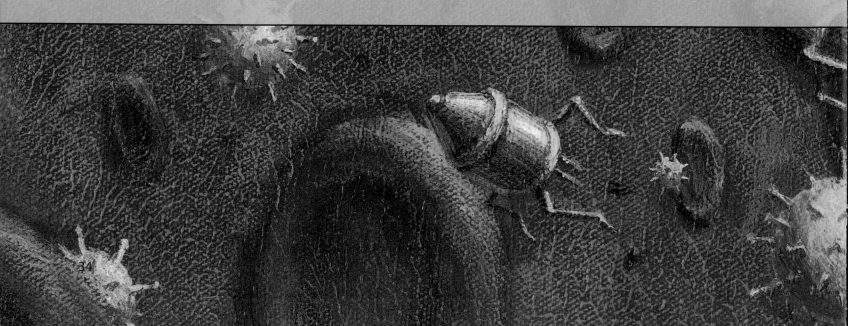

Nature's nanotechnology

Imagine something the size of a grain of salt. Now imagine something 500 000 times smaller. This is the realm of nanotechnology.

Nanotechnologists are working to create smaller-than-small devices and structures that will transform the world. Some of their wild ideas include coatings that let cars bounce back from accidents; artificial photosynthesis for cheap, clean power; microscopic disease-destroying robots that roam your body; liquid armor; and even invisibility cloaks!

But before they can create these things, scientists have to figure out exactly how matter behaves in the nanoworld. The laws of physics that apply in the full-sized world don't always apply in the world of atoms and molecules. For example, when you let go of an apple, gravity makes it fall to the ground. But in the nanoworld, gravity is less powerful than the forces that make molecules stick together. So if you, shrunken to nano proportions, let go of a nano-sized apple, it might just stick to your hand. To complicate matters more, making things this small requires parts and tools that are even smaller.

Nanotechnologists are just beginning to tackle such problems, but nature has been manufacturing with molecules since life on Earth began. With that kind of experience, nature can probably teach us a thing or two about making machines so tiny you could fit a thousand of them side by side into the period at the end of this sentence.

Tiny nanobots may one day target viruses inside the human body.

It makes sense to farm the way nature farms. The wild prairie — one of nature's farms — contains a mixture of different plants. This mixture gives prairie plants the best chance of survival. Taller plants shade out weeds and protect shorter plants from the sun, while the roots of others hold down the soil and keep it moist. Some plants make nutrients for other plants. If a pest attacks, chances are only a few plant species, not the whole prairie, will be destroyed. Farmers can learn from nature and plant a mix of hardy native grains instead of a single grain crop. A mixed crop would require less water and fertilizer. The plants would take care of themselves, and only one or a few species would be destroyed by a pest attack, not the whole crop.

Littering the seabed are fist-sized nuggets, called nodules, that contain valuable metals such as manganese, nickel, copper and cobalt. But mining on the seabed is expensive and disruptive for the sea creatures who live there. So scientists are hoping to learn a few things from microbes that live on the nuggets. Certain microbes called *Bacillus* M1 have the ability to dissolve the metals from the nodules. Scientists hope they can adapt this technique to collect minerals in the sea and on land, or to reclaim metal from waste, such as dead batteries.

Wetlands act as nature's filters. When water enters a marsh, swamp or bog, the water percolates slowly through a dense network of reeds, cattails, sedges, duckweed and other plants. Thickly tangled roots and leaves filter out sediment and clean pollutants from the water, while microbes break down organic matter and recycle nutrients. Following nature's example, some factories and towns are now directing their wastewater into human-made marshes, where the water can meander for several months, allowing the marsh plants and microbes to work their magic.

Sustaining our future

For thousands of years, we humans have shaped our environment according to our own needs. We have cut down forests. We have replaced native plant life with huge fields of one type of crop, such as wheat. We have drilled and blasted to get at minerals and fossil fuels. But our hunger for trees, land, minerals and fuels is now taking its toll. Forests are in danger, crops require huge doses of fertilizers, and mineral exploration leaves behind a trail of pollution.

Compare this with nature, where plants and animals use only what they need — or suffer the consequences. For instance, if foxes in an area consume too many rabbits, the fox population might grow at first, but then drops off because there's not enough food to go around. As the fox population shrinks, the rabbit population recovers. Each population keeps the other in check.

In the past, humans moved to a new place when local resources became scarce. But now, the human population is so large and widespread, there's nowhere left to go. Like the plants and animals around us, we need to find, and live within the limits of, our place in the web of life.

Fox and rabbit populations keep each other in balance.

Nature, the teacher

From one point of view, our future looks a little scary. Over the last few centuries, we've forgotten that we're just one of millions of species that live on Earth. In shaping the world for our use, we've stopped living in balance with the other creatures that share the planet. We've used too much stuff and created too much waste.

But there's good news — solutions are all around us. They are embedded in the structure of a maple seed, the shape of a bird's beak and the color of a butterfly's wing. All we have to do is look and learn.

A growing number of scientists, engineers, architects and business people are exploring, discovering and adapting nature's solutions to fix our own problems. Imagine machines that use only sun for energy. Imagine factories that manufacture biodegradable materials and recycle all their waste. Imagine farms that are pest resistant and self-fertilizing. Some day, these dreams may become a reality, using nature as a model. The more we copy nature, the more likely we will fit in with the rest of the species on this planet.

The biomimicry movement is growing, as humans realize just how much nature has to teach us. "Doing it nature's way" promises to change the world — in a good way.

Glossary

Amino acids: Small molecules that are the building blocks of proteins

Antibiotics: Drugs that kill microbes

Autism: A brain disorder that affects the way people experience the world around them; autistic children may have trouble expressing themselves or interacting with other people

Bacteria: Microscopic life forms made up of a single cell

Biomimicry: A way of thinking that uses nature as a model for developing ideas, processes and technologies

Camouflage: A strategy some animals and people use to hide objects, including themselves, by blending in with the surrounding environment

Center of gravity: The point in any object around which its weight is evenly distributed

Decompose: Rot; break up into basic components

DNA: Deoxyribonucleic acid — the molecule in every cell of a plant or animal that tells the cell what to do

Ecosystem: A community of living things that interact with one another and with the nonliving things in their environment

Emissions: Substances released into the air; often refers to pollutants from engines or industrial processes

Enzymes: Special proteins that bring molecules together to start or speed up chemical reactions

Evolve: To change gradually over time

Fiber optics: Technology that uses very thin glass or plastic fibers to transmit information in the form of light

Fossil fuels: Nonrenewable sources of energy (coal, oil, natural gas) that formed from the remains of prehistoric plants and animals

Global warming: An increase in the temperature at the earth's surface due to natural causes or human activity

Hydrogen: A colorless, odorless gas that may be used as a nonpolluting source of energy

Immune system: A collection of cells and organs that protects the body from disease

Iridescent: Having a shimmery, rainbow-like appearance that changes depending on your viewing angle

Microbes: Organisms so small they can only be seen through microscopes

Molecules: Groups of atoms with defined characteristics

Nanotechnologists: Scientists or engineers who work on nanotechnology

Nanotechnology: The study, design and production of useful devices ranging in size from several atoms to several hundred atoms

Organic matter: Material from living or once-living organisms that is capable of decay

Organisms: Living things

Photosynthesis: The process used by green plants and certain other organisms to convert carbon dioxide and water into sugars and oxygen using energy from sunlight

Predators: Animals that eat other animals

Prey: Animals that are eaten by other animals

Proteins: Large molecules made of long, folded-up chains of amino acids that carry out important tasks in living things

Sustainable communities: Groups of organisms that take only the resources they need from their environment, ensuring that they leave enough resources for future generations

Transistors: Electronic components that control the flow of electric current

Index